BEAUCOUP HAIKU

(and divergent verse)

by **Al Beck**

LORIEN HOUSE

P O BOX 1112   BLACK MOUNTAIN, NC   28711

This book is dedicated to
the eight thousand-plus
students who, over the
past forty years, have
taught me so much.

Beaucoup Haiku

Contents

BEAUCOUP HAIKU , other than its Forward
and Introduction, has been separated into
seven sections. It would be both unwieldy and,
as a matter of fact, useless to identify each
haiku/senryu by name (although several do
have identifiable titles). And for that reason,
also, the few non-haiku/senryu poems are not
listed here either; but fall easily into one of the
seven sections. Initially I thought it might be fun
to verbally play with the writing divisions -
torment the reader with such identifications as
'kernels of cogitation and cajolery'.
(Had I become too serious with my writing?
Would the reader reject more substantive
notions?) Because the traditions of this form
begged me to remain cautious, the character of
the format is more functional than far-out and
foolish. If this decision gives the reader pause,
sensing my darker, conservative nature, well,
so be it.
Haiku/Senryu has taken on an international
mantle which seems to break away from the
traditional format. I have chosen to follow the
traditional 17 syllable-three line structure as
closely as possible. In some cases the 5-7-5
rhythm is abridged. Nevertheless, the original
Japanese character pretty much remains intact.

ii

haiku: poetry's
potato chip. listen for
the crunch. ask for more

you are a temple -

open and warm; known only

by those who visit

FORWARD With ACKNOWLEDGEMENTS

This book of poetry completes the last of
four published works which evolved from
early writings and drawings more than
two decades ago into material still steaming
with my mental breath only days before the
manuscript was mailed off to publisher
David Wilson at Lorien House.
There is a magic in the three-line, seventeen
syllable poetry form - a musical magic, if you
will, in which words are transformed into a
form of lyrical weaponry.
Traditionally the seasons, plants, animals,
indeed all nature, are (is) the inspiration for
Haiku/Senryu. I have broken with tradition
only in the respect that a portion of my poetry
deals with the *inner* nature of humankind.
I see this more and more in the contemporary
work of haiku poets on an international level.
The Reaction Reader Team gave a particularly
sensitive reading to my manuscript. Kudos!!
Dan Campagna, Renee Gorrell, Dick Holmes,
Nanci Schrieber-Smith, Bill Stipe and Sherry
Strong all provided me with invaluable insights.
Finally, the consummate genius of David A.
Wilson as Editor of Lorien House played
a pivotal role in Beaucoup Haiku's handsome
appearance.

INTRODUCTION: Thoughts On Form

The Haiku is a vest-pocket form of poetry.
Actually, not all are identified as Haiku. Senryu*
is a similar style which also appears in
Beaucoup Haiku. Both use the 17 syllable-three
line form. Both are diminutive without losing
their impact. In fact, these poems give definition
to elegant and penetrating thoughts about nature,
the seasons, and the human condition (senryu).
Their origins in the Japanese 5/7/5 ideal form,
now appear in a slightly more flexible,
internationally-practiced structure.
The distinction between haiku and senryu lies
in the former's focus on "what-when-where" -
whereas, senryu tends to express human
"who-what" ideas.

Terse Verse

Imagery in these miniature poems depends upon
contrasting and, simultaneously, complementary
expression. Irony, humor, satire, pathos...all the
range of observation is here. Beyond the ubiquitous
fortune cookie commentary, Haiku is a complicated
poetry form. As opposed to a prolonged video
production, it has single photographic image-impact.
In other words these poems intimate or imply rather
than narrate or report. The reader is charged with
the task of connecting and entering into the various

layers of meaning.
The impact may or may not be subtle.

• •

I believe I may be the first to use the word
"Flashpoint" as it refers to haiku/senryu poetry.
Flashpoint is a term identifying a series of haiku or
senryu where each poem has an attitude *unleashed*.
Select pieces would fall into this special category.
Definition:
<u>FLASHPOINT</u> is the recognition of ancient verbal
martial arts expressed through the haiku/senryu
poetry form. It is expression less like an explosion
than an incision. "Sound Bites" are contemporary
commercial corruptions of the Flashpoint concept.

*This form was originally introduced to me by David Priebe,
Editor, Haiku Headlines, a publication in which several of the
poems in this book have been previously published. Four
others appeared in my books, Gnomes & Poems, Sight Lines
and Songs From The Rainbow Worm.

With Regard To The Drawings
I am reminded of the overwhelming positive impact
Nature has had in our lives and the influence those
humans who intrude [inflict?] upon that propinquity.
Sometimes, when I am most fortunate, my drawings
will evolve making synergistic metaphor on a different
level. And when it doesn't work, I shrug my shoulders
and persevere.

Nature's Voices /
Nature's Choices

dead limb with twigs like

bony fingers. hey branch!

we've all seen better days.

listen to dawn's

fragile footsteps - tango on

the horizon. Olé!

first snow; surface for

poets' peculiar songs.

wild turkey leaves tracks, too

front paws work by instinct.

sharp claws extended, cat

builds nest in my lap.

perched on a gutter's

edge above the feeder,

chickadee waits its turn.

old path cut through the woods -

overgrown. Nature abhors

human trespass.

squirrel-nibbled nut fragments

strew the deck! no table manners

in treetops!

like gunshot, flawed nuts

rejected - hammer the roof.

persnickety squirrels!

pond edge - frog's safe leap

from cat-pounce; takes drink instead.

some compensation!

audacious bird and

meandering moth - brief fluttering -

no contest.

strange dog - expressed

friendship or territory rights -

pissing on my tires?

licking me while their

claws dig in. seems cats have

ambivalent feelings.

we live in the

corridor between earth and sky -

sunshine and shadows.

when will stars all say

goodbye; space wrapped in a

sea of final light? Howl.

brightness penetrates

forest from the west: silhouettes

rake a sunset.

white cat is motionless,

suffused in sounds of twilight:

cricket chatter.

woodland quiet

interrupted by distant rumble -

God clears His throat.

rain massages

naked silence - a moist mantra

for meditation.

umbrella for scattered showers

wind's voice deepens -

races through the hollow.

oak trees improvise a dance.

unfurls his web, spans

unguarded spaces. spider

twirls; part acrobat

fish with scales

there's music in the

silence of a pristine wood:

squirrels dance on tiptoes.

Mozart sound soars through

our unconscious - eagle drifts

high in an updraft.

sun's snowy white flesh

emerges through morning fog.

flushes out goldfinch.

wounded bird, huddled

in pain, draped with obligation,

tries to take wing.

who sees the pond more

precisely - a surveying hawk

or frog-hunting cat?

cat sits below bird

feeder pretending he's a

hairy rock. (it twitched).

prancing through high grass

extraordinary deer

improvise arabesques.

rabbits dart across -

challenging my headlights:

libido out of control.

Oak trees' green leaves stroke

a lean blue sky. Cool breeze

tickles the butterfly.

wind announces its

arrival, scuffling the trees -

like bedroom slippers.

summer-lazy cat

snoozing. Hey! Furry-Goya-Maja,

what a pose!

full moon reflects

sun's juicy glory;

ripe white fruit so transitory.

Red fox with a dead

bunny in its mouth; there is quick

and there's quicker.

Two foolish fawns

gambol along the back road.

Where's their mother sleeping?

Relentless Downy

Woodpecker checks each shagbark

crevice. What hustle!

chickadee flutters

at the feeder. retreats to

sun-drenched sycamore.

hawk circles the hollow

in delicate silence -

shapes sky-mandalas

wind licks its way through

hickory, oak, sugar maple -

tasty, these leaves.

cool morning air -

at my ear, early rising

mosquito's last whine. . .Smack!

spider's web camouflaged

by autumn morning fog.

there's lace on my face.

finch at the feeder

cat purrs in my lap - together

we greet the dawn.

Silence in the woods

broken - blue jays jabber.

Soft edge of a new day.

long shadows at sunrise

fawn hock-high in dew soaked grass -

sweet, sweet freedom!

still dawn gathers light -

as pond swiftly ripples. grass

carp breaks the surface.

full moon: reflected

light, golden eye, shadow

maker, tide's appetite.

stars - gemstones on the

blanket called sky. . . or maybe

holy graffiti

observe nature's

melody - moonlight never

forgets its performance.

dance under a thin roof

with closed eyes. hear the rain's

generous applause.

steady rain whets the

appetite, like verbal

foreplay, for nostalgia.

blending wild blackberries,

pectin and sugar:

cosmic-delicious jam!

white cat crouches, unseen by

squirrel, masked from sparrow's

sight. instinct in charge

Skink in a bowl still

wriggling. I thought it was dead.

Here's the door, brave skink!

search for signs:

in flowers' wilted truth; in bones

of a beautiful beast.

Nature's cosmic fragments

float through our winter woods.

The wind is hungry.

early bird gets badly designed

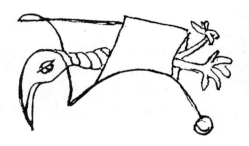

full moon pours splendid

radiance on fresh snow -

landscape in gourmet's glow.

discovered leaf portrait

A WALK IN LIFE'S WOODS

I stepped gingerly through
the churlish underbrush
down steep glades of
cheap whine and limp excuses;

past gaunt trees long dead -
nature's brittle bones
flaunting death in the fetid air -
now houses for day drowsing owls,
themselves safe from curiosity's
gnarled fingers, and beyond
the cynic's snare.

I turned aside from savage passageways
guarded by pompous huffpuffers
undaunted by their righteous moan
and lethal stare.

sudden sun's rays, like slim limbs
of a young child streaked onto
undiscovered soil - flashing feet,
they struck into new ground
urging me to follow the fresh sound.
such sunlight music suggested I learn
to distinguish the "coulds" from the "can'ts".

a walk in a tired old woods was
my time to try a different dance.

in this part of the country
where seasons with tangled
intentions have difficulty
making up their minds until
it's too late,
spring is occasionally
passed by; and in the process,
we are confused about what
happened to our body's clock.

• • •

moonlight brushpaints the

footprints of woodland creatures -

shadow and silver.

diving digit
confronts flying crescent as they
discuss extinction

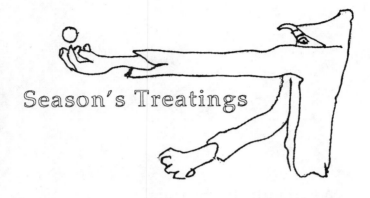

Season's Treatings

Corrugated cloud

layers ripple March skies.

Winter packs it in. Ciao!

quiet sequestered

cold, cloudy March days; seeds ache

for germination

March rains fill the bucket

used to water spring seedlings

in our window.

silly robin

assumed spring began mid-March

alights in fresh snow. Brrrrr!

horny beast blossom

Spring stroll in

uncharted woodlands -

expect the inevitable tick

Out in early April sun -

jacket zipped. Safe from

winter's last cool kiss.

At last! April's red bud

blossoms. Cat's frozen pose:

waiting for a skink.

mid-April groundfrost.

spring can't seem to drag itself

out of bed - me too.

smart, these May apples:

late April risers, sporting

their own umbrellas.

new green leaves flashed

by May's spring moon - flushed when told

they look lovely tonight.

Mind merges with flesh

remembers voices of rain.

June is so juicy.

daylilies return:

every color and design.

summer friends - briefly.

August is spiderweb

season: worn woodland paths

set with woven traps.

flurry of feathers:

woodpecker lands on feeder.

breakfast is now served.

glowing soybean fields.

autumn takes its deepest breath

as summer expires.

sugar maple,

autumn dressed - undisguised

conspicuous consumption.

September storm coming -

late night lightning flashes.

fireflies can't compete.

morning strokes Missouri

with September's scattered

showers. Earth tastes limp.

Sunday dawns. no

ripple on the pond; chatterless

air. September yawns.

early April and

late September are married

to the same Ol' Man.

with tangled intentions,

September suffers from

internal bruises.

first frost. last flower

on the vine is lost. it has

no survival skills.

winter's first fond embrace -

yet a trace of autumn

auburn on her face.

soft chartreuse, electric

yellow, orange fire, raw mauve,

wrinkled brown . . . . leaves.

red ribbons tied to

every tree - big party?

maybe November's leaves.

In these October

years, I'm the regal

fritillary butterfly

= = =

momentarily

mounted on purple coneflower

at season's end.

winter strains at

November's leash - aches to romp

untethered; bares its teeth

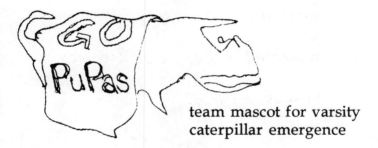

team mascot for varsity
caterpillar emergence

December trees; dark fingers

scrape near-night gray sky -

(smell snow in the air?)

woodpecker rattles . . .

November's twig-fingers rake

the sudden sunrise.

mute-orange, ochre,

maroon; November tree-music

sotto voce.

frigid January

morning in the flood of

a full moon: cats preen.

January's wind

gnashes its teeth. Trees with less

temper in their limbs.
- - - - - - - -
branch-bones moan and ache;

by some life sustaining

miracle do not break.

vertiginous leaf

on branch, still flutter-dances

in February.

February full moon

drapes over bone bare trees

like some archangel.

Learner and Labyrinth

learn to walk uncharted

reality without

stepping on landmines.

unconventional

thinking discourages a

sense of mental sloth.

imagination

is roadkill on traditional

learning highways

if fish had vocabulary

two words they wouldn't

know: dry and fry.

teach with matches

and candle. urge learners

light it - to search dark places.

teacher is resource

for the resonance of a

student's own music.

high noon.

pity the sleepy pedagogue

who believes it's still daybreak.

students must be

accountable to themselves.

teachers are guides not gods.

ICONOCLAST

if middle management

dislikes my idea,

it's certain to work.

incompetent leaders

play head games with us;

squeeze out their mental pus.

successful teachers

arm students to lob ideas

like hand grenades

some teachers retire

prematurely concurrent

with teaching classes.

the learner-teacher
relationship: a very
delicate balance

Life combines working

with the right tools and learning

how to suffer fools.

listen to education's

circumscribed, byzantine

politics growl.

Dismantle

originality. Memorize

dates. Brain-dead wisdom.

within the teaching

technician's shadow, we lose

student connection.

dark ordeal: middle

management's transfiguration

of guile to bile.

conventional tactic

to proselytize didactic:

tyranny.

Live the Present.

Plan for Future's dream-bubble

Cast grief in Past's rubble.

to learn, never smile -

only sweat; a new generation

vulcanized.

indignant politicians

who claim they can't be bought

haven't been caught.

wrestle ritual -

ignore internal injury.

myth is on fire!

without passion's flint,

intellect has the impact

of rain-soaked fireworks.

The choice is always

yours: fresh words from your lips

or old wind from your ass.

Epiphany comes

to many during moments

of desperation.

not so much what you

learn that counts but how you

feel about what you know.

something compelling

about a lost cause: the

impetuous inspired

The worthy fool

enjoys sudden good fortune

noiselessly.

Guilt comes in raising

children by being mostly

right some of the time.

with sudden soulful

revelation or affectionate touch,

tears teach.

reincarnation

means relearning places I

can and cannot scratch.

age asks us: choose to

learn new things or try hangin'

onto what we know.

Myth rises to a

lifestyle deeper than our

daily experience.

school's preconceived limits:

coloring book tradition -

kids "color in".

Problems' answers are

not yet found; so search for one

still unasked question.

Epiphany - divine

experience - happens

when the time is right.

my point is - one gets

on a bike to ride, not to

presume he'll fall off.

History teaches:

never look back at barriers

or burials.

distinguish

Definition from Label:

grape juice from crayon color

three things are dangerous

to learning: rote, ritual

and fear of risk.

listening very

carefully we touch the words

with mental fingers.

Look hard - understand.

Look too hard - become

liberated, skeptical

it happened during the summer of '54

dumb luck found me in Taegu, Korea.

In the war he had made captain,

category - battlefield commission,

and I remained an awestruck corporal

mesmerized by his story of capture,

torture and escape from the enemy.

I clenched my fists, "Were you ever in pain?"

He shaped a dry, wry smile at my question.

"My hands were tied behind me at the wrists,"

he sighed, "the other end of the long rope was

draped over a tree limb. I was pried up until

only my toe tips touched ground. . . left there

 to cope until morning." "But how could you

endure the pain?" I cried. The question barely

a grope to hide the image from my mind.

"Soldier," he quietly responded,

"I learned to love the rope."

SURVIVOR

I am a survivor from the land of pedantry
where inhabitants constantly   lick themselves.
preening is their primary pleasure.

unlike Socrates who used questions
(no, not on midsemester tests),
learning was defined there as a ritualistic treasure.

If one is having fun in school he failed to understand.
"This is no game, young man" they said.
But it is a game and a deadly one

where winners alter their shape
to interfere with natural soul work and
each candidate now performs a role

in order to adhere to rules exceedingly complex.
To be a true survivor, it takes creative grit,
a gentle sense of humor to avoid becoming victim

and one, just one particular dictum:
don't ever put up with any of their shit.

knock on Logic's door

enter with intuition

in the form

of a vessel

of a function

of a thought

of a ritual

of a language

of a culture

of a spirit.

leave -

with your myth on fire.

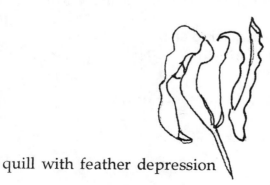

quill with feather depression

scanning the alien mind

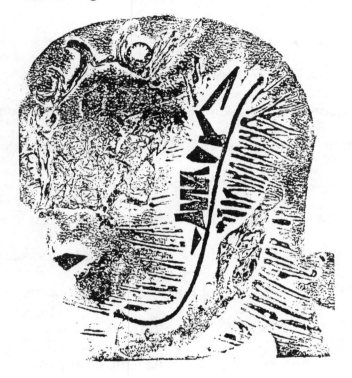

untie the wounded

butterfly. give wings to the

wisdom: grow or die

BIRTHDAY POEM
FOR CHRISTOPHER, YEAR ONE

What is it like to be one year old?

Well, walking gets easier, I've been told.

And since I have lived through all four seasons once,

I prefer weather dry (like my diapers....I'm no dunce)

Of course, recently new molars grew in

giving me reasons to loudly protest 'til I got so hoarse

that the new words I have in my limited vocabulary

sound a bit cuckoo and what's even more scary

I've begun to believe what Mom's saying is true:

Life'll get more complex by the time I am two!

subterranean value judgements

Harmony, Discord
and Creative Spirit

a scowl is the wrong

vessel to launch onto your

journey through the day.

a fertile step: I

look into her eyes - see

the charm beneath the skin.

without change, a gift

inside us remains unwrapped,

unseen and untouched.

HAIKU TRIPLET ON LUCK

tools and attitude
are wings on the same bird.
it's called Preparation.

••

Luck is when a
Preparation bird snatches
worm Opportunity.

••

when Opportunity
worm falls into the bird's nest,
it's called Dumb Luck.

definition for extraordinary luck:
3 needles from 3 different haystacks

with curtains of

circumstance one can do

nothing about - persevere.

now and then creative

genius bears no fruit - sad

for society.

by Draconian

design - with retirement,

weekdays lose character.

feel Age-animal

rub against us, pleading

to be fed. He's bleeding.

daily exercises done.

at my age - permission

given to moan.

the Techno-man's voice

resonates evolution:

grunt to gigabyte.

arrogance is the

virus of youth; meanspirit:

plague for the mature.

negative thoughts are

dry seeds in arid soil -

food for desperate birds.

tears are the

spontaneous gift, the

metaphor of abject sorrow.

depression sucks the

marrow from mental bones:

cavalier attitude.

soul craves kind words more

than body needs dessert; and. . . .

they're calorie-free!

without the stranger

among us, it's not possible

to see ourselves.

Grandson visits - room

filled with undeniable

continuity.

strange child waves - not to

acknowledge me but to show

she knows how to wave.

falling in love

generates its own lack of

specific gravity.

puzzle pieces are

manufactured. the perfect

marriage is a lie.

whatever else is

said, relationships die if

not constantly fed.

perfect people

wisely indulge each other's

temper and bad habits.

first light: mind ready

to take on the day; body

stubbornly resists.

exercise. . . muscles strained.

no mind over this matter:

it's belly fat.

LAZY AS AN ART FORM, Part One

Not moved to rise from

bed; but with something to do

if I did get up.

pick at mental scabs

from a bad night's sleep. expose

raw wounds to daylight.

wise person is less

agitated with haunting

thoughts than stone in shoe.

humor self-perpetuates.

bodies in motion

ignore gravity.

phrase first coined by ancient,

angry, constipated poet:

Bowels of Hell.

sarcasm - lively

language falling into parched

conversations.   Yeah.

"Give us this day our

daily brethren" - (Sign at the

Cannibal Cafe).

lip of adult life -

sixteen; still speaking mostly

social gibberish.

judgement is drink for

the court's universe, builder's

burden, cynic's curse.

compulsive cleaner

drives me daffy. no hiding

from The Grim Sweeper.

who protects one's own

butt at another's expense

claims the millstone prize.

Betrayal emerges

from Truth's shadow; briefly

gleams before it dies.

sin Moses had no

room to carve on his stone

tablets: self-deception.

avoid riding two

mean and nasty horses:

Mendacity and Sloth.

bad attitude

who can give what you

forbid yourself? (genetic

predisposition).

some people choose to

be perpetually spaced -

known as human waste.

drawn into the pattern

of life is inevitably

death's motif.

Perfection flies in

reality's face.   All Persian

rugs have one flaw.

Fear is Risk's elusive

Shadow Queen: Mantra for

the Mediocre.

comfortable shoes

lose their credibility

worn with wrinkled socks.

mermaids, even, have

travail - with sudden sore throats

or cramps in the tail.

blowing on hot tea

fogs my glasses. blowing my

own horn fogs my mind.

Fool! Don't sit in ashes

of discontent; go write

new poetry.   Fly!

Life's swim? . . . worth noting:

brains or brawn don't count without

serious floating.

mental acuity's a blade

well-honed, slashing through

babble-worn bone.

just turned right, should have

been left. no fog here, except

in my mind.

like constipated worms -

artists without intuition

are worthless.

radical advice

one gives to all young artists:

put feat to your fire!

I'll write poems driving

the backland. One hand holds

wheels on blacktop, mostly.

one day tyrants' smiles,

like broad swords, may decapitate

dreams; - not today.

beneath Time's mountain -

this illusion of distance.

Youth rides a fast horse.

fools are flowers

thinking they'll never die.

we wrinkle dry for display.

eyes open, body

still. can she hear? Coma:

cloud-world, disconnected.

seated here in a

more lucid moment; (so why

are my eyes open?)

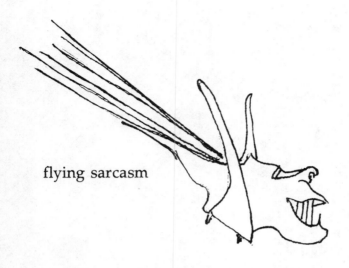

flying sarcasm

consider the

enormity of life lived

without conformity.

Life's 4-R challenge:

choose between Rhythm,

Ritual, Routine or Rut

curiosity:

mystic fire - deep under -

just around - behind that . . .

swill or sermon may

determine inspiration

or indigestion.

Driving the lefthand lane -
Nashville highway sign
reads "Two People Minimum
Per Vehicle In This Lane"
I'm confused.

If two think people's total
weight in car A, say, is 210;
but car B has one big bubba
at 285... Oh, you tell me,
"weight's not the issue."

Well, how about if bubba
has a spaniel sitting next to him
(seatbelt on, of course)?
Hmm.."only people" you insist.
OK, then, what about you and me?

We're both wearing a size D-neck,
V-neck shirt; live in Teaneck which,
admittedly, is minimally scenic.
Now wait! you say there's "only
one person in this vehicle?"

Doesn't it count
if I'm schizophrenic?
TALK
TO
ME!

Elvis quadruped impersonator

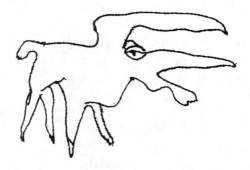

HOLIDAY CRUTCH

Today's social liturgy, posing as
sacrosanct, is designed for deceit or fake
in the land of silk and money. Yes,
I mean, for goodness sake Yuletides
now compete with store shelf stuff
for Halloweens. And it's not so funny.

Much more to the point,
if Truth be revealed,
we are hermetically sealed
into culture's secular customs
with minimal authentic emotion.
To add to that notion,

every credit card carrying
automaton needs an attitude to shop.
Conventional messages from the
commercially pious intrude and
exclude our effort to stop the
practice of their philosophic bias

making it difficult to distinguish
the precious from the platitude.
When at five years old, in bed
I was put next to my stuffed furry
bear friend with his furry torn foot,
no gift, wrapped carefully, ever replaced

the goodnight kiss for both him and me.
And though now my friends are not so furry
and I'm described by some as 'longer in the tooth',
in my head I still can hear father reading me
poems from his youth. See, it's only personal ritual
which'll enrichen any holiday season.

This ceremonial paper-rite you are reading
has its unique reason. In a world where
high tech hype and feel-good drugs substitute
for human hugs and such, it makes considerable
sense for each of us to reach across the space
of Time's invisible crutch to keep in touch.

• • •

to prescribe an appropriate treatment

no matter how exact the dose is

apply an ample ration of pure compassion;

we'll label it "soul osmosis".

something on my mind

did you know. . .

pre-nose drops' invention:
dogs were trained to suck snot?

Past Condemned /
Past Celebrated

past and future

inexorably linked by

reheating leftovers.

our explosive youth

in retrospect: past condemned,

past celebrated.

because Time transforms

us, friends mellow into warm,

rare, vintage spirits.

lasting friendship blends

history behind us - made now

- yet to be written

I met a woman

ninety-three who did not look

her age: restlessness.

like germinating seeds

old secrets interrupt their way

through life's soil.

Death travels at no

specific speed; arrives on

foot or trotting steed.

old buffalo

forsaken - dismissed by

history's contentious plot.

some spirits create

a roaring sound; others don't.

History echoes both.

old age is a story

sundered: pages torn from

a familiar book.

like nested containers,

days fold into each other.

what dish remains?

at twilight, memories

burrow into crimson clouds'

succulent shadows.

Life's gracious banquet -

often raided by Time's

voracious appetite.

this year was two weeks long.

disrobed from its disguise reveals

Time hiccuped.

memory is

History's song - skewed by a few

dissonant voices.

Though dreams appear long,

most occur in seconds. Time

is a false prophet.

History is not

Truth, but perceptions from the

last person standing.

if Truth be revealed:

what Adam got from the snake

was a tomato.

passion constantly

scratches History's persistent itch

. . . . Art, the ointment.

Elderly amateur

does Glenn Miller kitchen

fantasy dance.   Swish!

six inch glass dog

on young child's bureau -

just to look at, not cuddle.

precious years of youth

- money melts faster than a

January thaw.

king's father died these

many years ago. his words

still soar like a hawk.

detached from birth, I

hold this broken string. never

knew my grandfather.

may passing of our

human race thus be mourned by

those to replace us.

until her death, with

every breath - electric myth:

Princess Diana.

Time's perishable ring

is a circle in which

its core cannot hold.

analysts have no

reason to canonize Death.

It is beyond Truth.

recovered memory

transforms to darkside's

fantasy disclosure.

some are better at

nurturing nostalgia than

preparing their future.

Time's slippery speed best

measured by shower's soap bar

turning thin-slivered

memories of my

youth return as wounds with feelings

which make them bleed.

Beyond undefined
temptations at two
Past the sneer and
caterwaul of youth
in its fourteenth year

above several decades
dedicated to distinguish
winner from washout,
who doesn't understand
the sublime Struggle

- against all the odds -
to find the special time
and the soul-filled space
where we can converse
with the gods?

Botticelli's first attempt:
"Birth of Mabel"

From worn-out teddy bear

to bluejeans,

then, ultimately,

mind and muscle,

our shadow-dappled history

(celebratory as well as tragic)

is an amalgam of fragile mystery,

occasional noble accuracies and

sacred, spherical magic.

How we reconcile reason

with imagination is memory's

gracious miracle.

Human Designed
In Body & Mind

two keys unlock

Creative Life's gate: Passion

and Imagination.

Two a.m. - charged with

mental energy - wrong time

to get up and dance?

Kindness - a human craft

essential in friendship;

foundation for love.

music keeps us alive -

head to toe; possibly

an adagio.

think like a teapot

to create a teapot - pour

your heart into it.

clay spirits cry out.

we listen with our fingers

for Passion's response.

Culture's Truth is most tasty

when served from vessels

of uncommon clay.

art, as opiate, provides

thoughtful metaphor

with perverse pleasure.

cynicism is

bright apple with worm inside.

it's there - we're certain.

Reason's voice is

muted by brutal fingers.

Anger has a harsh hand.

try to remember:

fault lies not in forgetting

but in not caring.

Deceit is tasteless;

but is the feel of dry oak leaves

by the handful.

Art - precious gift - lives

side-by-side with the beast

in us all. Miracle.

courage and imagination

protect us from

Medusa's danger.

anticipating

new adventure, Risk sometimes

wears a dirty shirt.

chase exhilarates

more than the capture - defines

a creative life.

elderly underwear -

soil it or spend quality

time on toilet.

Growing older, my

mind seems more alienated

from its body.

birth may be no picnic

still, it's more painful to

let go at eighteen

creature who looks behind
while stumbling forward

glorious events

occur through chemistry of

planning and pure chance.

imagination's

power will raise us up from

conventional mud.

music draws our deeper breath

warm thoughts flicker -

new logs on an old fire.

When silence tastes like

dry bread, dip in digestible

conversation.

Like rodents' aimless scurry,

words rose from dark tunnels

of sleeplessness.

anger in my writing.

I use the dictionary

like a hammer.

twisted sorrows turn

to stones. lose control. lose heart.

find soul - in my bones.

this poet survives

in deep woods with strong back, weak

stomach and loose mind.

Like a kite set loose

in high wind, free unforgiving

thoughts. Catharsis.

insult one unworthy

of scorn. with whom do you share

satisfaction?

greatest art's danger

is in its lure to nurture

our common darkness.

alternative lifestyles,

as opposed to a real job:

poet. . . artist.

voice of the Muse

crisply commands; submissively

I serve her pleasure.

liberal tolerance

persuades us to cautiously

include the prude.

beasts born in dreaded

dark, encounter shadows we

worship cheerfully.

Sick - is billions of

lies and deceptions supporting

our universe.

sadness

Fear's shape,   buried

comfortably in shadow,   turns

mere rain to sheer pain

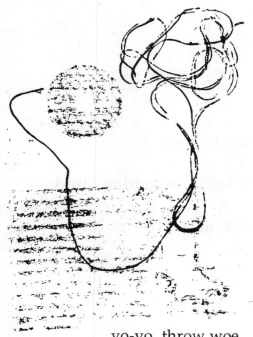

yo-yo throw woe

Love between Dad and

me - detached - precious cup on

high shelf out of reach.

mid-life crisis is

defined as becoming blind,

deaf and really dumb.

Acknowledging Appetite, Instinct, Ambiguity, Expectations & Energy

Great Leaps often occur

for frogs, flames and

occasionally for faith.

important as it

is to dream, sometimes it's wise

to read directions.

No delicate

disposition this beast - Hope

is a hungry tiger.

eyeball to eyeball -

contest with Evolution.

look! there! Instinct blinked!

rock star's absurd scream

drowns piano pounding -

fine way to treat Steinway.

to live a long and

healthy life, light your cigarette

in a high wind.

Reflection is Fortune's

yearning for overindulgence:

Icarus.

make marks in wet cement

step out before it hardens

into lament.

when memory deepens

conviction, it contaminates

the future.

what's fair is often

a state of mind. compassion

leaves revenge behind.

insomnia's no

hacking cough; it's mental pig

digging in the trough.

hungry beast, Anger,

streaks across soul's sacred soil

searching for its feast.

character strength unlike

Gordian knots decays -

heroes unravel.

moon, stroke my belly.

let someone else bay a while.

coyote retired.

holding up my madness

to the mirror - defy

curiosity.

persistence - a force

reaching into soul beyond

our understanding.

Trickster says: "to live

a lie, by ripple-effect,

one must swallow it."

what we want and what

we treasure are diff'rent tunes

with diff'rent measure.

under the stars or

asleep in bed, dreams seldom

arrive on horseback.

inspiration is

seductive. submissively

accommodate her.

dreams are mystic wisdom

racing reality -

running in bare feet.

to distinguish

inspiration from obsession,

listen to the clay.

Wise person once said,

"All warriors die - some in

battle, some in bed."

Life's unholy secret blend

of luck and limitations -

go figure.

sheep in an unsuccessful
attempt to disguise itself
as a potato

Passion to create

is not preferable but

unavoidable.

while you reach for a

new brass ring, celebrate your

seat on that Big Swing.

Play! Sing! or Dance!

with wine, word and fiddle!

(dum-ditty-diddle-diddle)

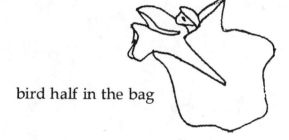

bird half in the bag

Art, grounds for lean suggestion,

entertains with tastes

of indigestion.

liberated from

youth's ego focus, graciousness

moves me to tears.

To transcend limitations,

laugh at miracles,

dance without music.

indispensability

is beyond worth. it's

an intoxicant.

intimacy and

identity are the eyes

of companionship.

roar of mountain storms

or meadow's light rain: anger's

difference from chagrin.

From larva's sins

pupa begins; and in the end

Prometheus wins.

Reality's

reconstruction transpires through

sacred struggle called Change.

hard-pressed to distinguish

atrophy from dogma,

they dress near alike.

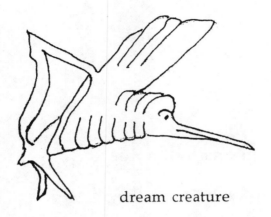

dream creature

larger pattern holds

life's fabric together;

even us looser threads.

for Father's Day, son

build me a world where energy

improves with age.

THE HALF-WOMAN

Now, twenty one years late,
the lady with a half-body
who would navigate the demands
of hill-town Cortona, Italy
still haunts me.
She propelled forward with her hands,
pushing up on her palms through the pain
- face strained with history's crude cruelty
- waist thumping a measured paduana
on the worn gray cobblestoned streets.
Dust from time-worn handcart wheels
rose with each body thrust and thud.
Two thousand B.C. Etruscans
had built this city with ninety foot high walls
...plumb, mind you. One old woman crawls -
a modern living metaphor how Roman soldiers
sliced off Cortona's life from the belly down
so many centuries before.

Pretentiousness is a soft
center of the shadow bag;

it dresses up the vaunted hero
and dresses down the haughty hag.

In Life's velvet shadows -

reality never seen.

What's the password?

Try hard. Do your best.

Nurture healthy levels of

dissatisfaction.

emotional luxuries
one can never afford:

• good short term memory

• romances ignored

• enough chocolate
   to fill the hall

• and one more indulgence
   I cannot recall

unlike the builder,
priest or hunter,
coyote may not be
grist for social glue.

his primary role is, as
shadow's voice, distinguishing
machine from maniac;
mythic from possibly true;

dreamer from drudge;
spirit from substance;
winged from the rooted,
trapped in reality's goo.

not hopes nor dreams, but

promises we make ourselves

get us in trouble

inevitably

progress preys on apathy

and posterity.

Second Thoughts

self-control: bridging

the gap between featherbrained

and simpleminded

peripatetic

iconoclast am I, who

sleeps with mental snakes.

Long John Foo-Bird

resolve Life's doubts:

use the alchemy how we

feel about what we know.

vision's Truth is

generally a crutch. distance

is more smell than touch.

FINAL THOUGHTS:
Making My Own Medicine

If we are to be content with the world in which
we live as a reflection of our technological and
analytical prowess, is it enough? Will we truly be
reflecting the human condition? Is that all there is?
Are we happy living in a world knowing only
about its physical character?
My mind fills with questions, searching for the
most instructive one which will pin-point the reason
I write poetry, make pottery, draw, design, listen to
Mozart and James Taylor, celebrate the symbol, the
metaphor and nurture the mysteries of nature in my
musings. The soul truly suffers if we accept analysis
and reason as our only human resources. As I implied
in the Forward to my second book of poetry and drawing,
Sight Lines, inspiration continues to be a mystical aspect
of human energy. Combine it with a love for language,
some synectic playfulness and occasionally the results
can be unexpectedly delicious.

Finally, to paraphrase a fine artist/educator and friend,
George Kokis: Poetry-making is healing - but the cure
must be repeated again and again. We all need this
ritual curing of the psychic fabric - of the individual
and the society. It makes us pliable, malleable, supple,
limber and more tender. Better able to perform our
various functions. More respectful of the differences in
others. Making poetry is making obsessional ideas
conscious; thus dissolving their hold on you.

Poetry-making is learning to make your own medicine.

ABOUT THE AUTHOR

In 1956, an intellectually indifferent
Northwestern University graduate
(art major), still freshly fragrant from
his U.S. Army tour of Korea, packed his
knapsack, picked up his guitar and sailed
for Paris, France.
Now, over four decades later, retired
from an iconoclastic teaching career and
four published poetry books later, he
continues to remain "vertical - taking
nourishment regularly" and writes:

> I have been careless
> with Time; still searching for where
> my light is buried.

(photograph taken in Paris, 1957, for
publicity by the United States Information
Service as Beck was hired to go on a folk-
singing tour throughout France)

BOOKLIST

"Al Beck is witty, playful, and having fun with words. If comparisons are fruitful, some of these poems reminded me of a giddy Ogden Nash."
- Dr. Sam Grabarski

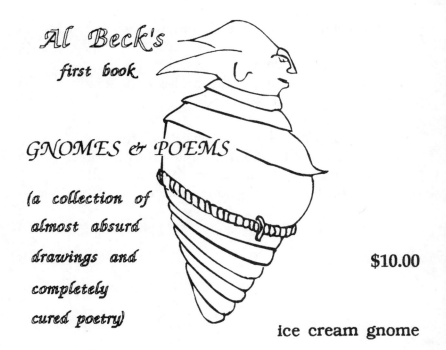

Al Beck's
first book

GNOMES & POEMS

(a collection of
almost absurd
drawings and
completely
cured poetry)

$10.00

ice cream gnome

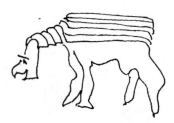

misfiled material beast